LET'S INVESTIGATE

BEING AN INVENTOR

© 1992 by Heinemann Library, A Division of

All rights reserved. No part of this publication may be reproduced, stored in a retrieval system, or transmitted in any form or by any means, electronic, mechanical, photocopying, recording, or otherwise, without prior permission of the copyright holder.

ISBN 0 7105 0968 0

Printed and bound in R.O.A.

Published in this edition by Peter Haddock Ltd, Pinfold Lane, Bridlington, East Yorkshire YO16 5BT

© 1997 Peter Haddock Ltd/Geddes & Grosset Ltd

ISBN 07105 0968 5

Printed and bound in India

PART ONE

HANDY MAN

It is our inventive instinct that has allowed us human beings to survive as long as we have. In physical terms, in terms of strength, speed and resilience, we have always come a poor second to the rest of the animal kingdom and should have long since fallen victim to it. But it is not for nothing that the earliest example of a 'true' human has been designated *Homo habilis*, or 'Handy Man'.

It has been estimated that if the age of the earth-moon system (say 4,700 million years) is likened to a single year, Handy Man only came on the scene (some two million years ago) on 31 December—and not until half-past eight in the evening at that. He invented the wheel at about one minute to midnight.

This last event occurred somewhere between 10,000 and 3000 BC. What, then, had human beings been doing in the meantime? Primarily they had been evolving, from gibbering beasts to ones able to think, to rationalise. The earth was a dangerous place. There were extremes of temperature that human beings were no longer built to take. They had to find a natural shelter, or build an artificial one. This, in turn, had to be kept warm and protected from wild animals. By 235,000 BC, Chellean, or early Stone Age, man in Europe, had found *one* answer to *both* these problems—a good fire.

What was more, fire had a third great blessing to bestow on its first masters. It enabled them to cook. Suddenly, after two million years, humans were able to consume all kinds of meat and vegetation that, in their raw state, had been inedible. The first hot meal must have been a welcome change.

THE LEVER

If fire was Stone Age man's most significant 'discovery', the lever was his greatest invention proper. It gave him his first mechanical advantage over nature. It allowed him to move loads that were beyond his own strength. In theory, this advantage was unlimited. Archimedes was right when he said, several thousand years later, that, given a sufficiently long lever and a fixed point to stand on somewhere in space, he could shift the very Earth. The principle he had in mind is illustrated in figure 1.

Figure 1: Principle of the lever

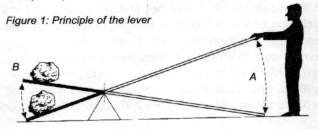

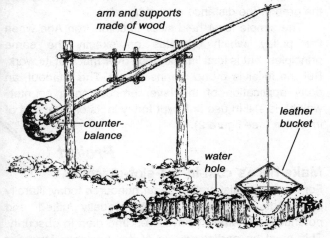

arm and supports
made of wood

counter-
balance

leather
bucket

water
hole

In this case the white arm of the lever (extending from the point of leverage, or fulcrum, to the man) is *twice* as long as the black one. Therefore, in practice, it will enable its user to move a boulder *twice* as efficiently— i.e. it will double his strength. However, nature demands a price for this 'advantage'. The white arm must be moved through an arc *twice* as long as that asked of the black one. Thus A = 2 x B. If the power arm were increased to 10 times the length of the load arm, its user would only require a tenth of his strength, but the equation would then read A = 10 x B, and so on. In short, the longer the power arm, the greater its efficiency and the greater the distance it must travel.

The simple lever held sway until the Iron Age when the pulley, which operates on exactly the same principles, but is less limited, took over much of its work. But the lever is by no means extinct. The shadouf, an early application of the lever embodying a counter-weight, is still in use in Egypt today in its original role of irrigation (*see* figure 2).

Project

Make Hero's coin-in-the-slot machine

For every scientist and engineer honoured today, literally thousands of others, perhaps equally gifted and potentially as famous, have lived and died in obscurity. This must be particularly so of the Ancients. However one man, Hero of Alexandria, who lived some time before the birth of Christ, saved himself and certain of his predecessors from this fate by recording their achievements in some detail.

Hero's coin-in-the-slot machine employs the lever in a fascinating way, and a careful study of its illustration (*see* figure 3) should enable you to build a replica. The original was housed in an urn and placed at the entrance to a temple. Here, seemingly by magic, it dispensed equal quantities of 'holy water'—at a price.

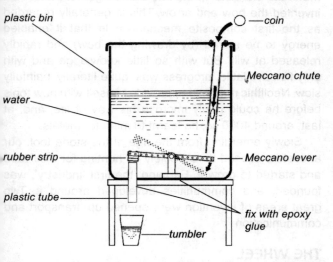

Figure 3 Hero's coin-in-the-slot machine—modern version

plastic bin

coin

Meccano chute

water

rubber strip

Meccano lever

plastic tube

fix with epoxy glue

tumbler

The lever is used rather like a seesaw. When a coin is placed in the *slot,* it rides down a *chute.* As it strikes one end of the lever, the plug attached to the opposite end is raised, allowing liquid to escape into a waiting tumbler. But only for a moment. As soon as the coin slides into the water, the lever rights itself and the plug is restored.

OUT OF THE STONE AGE

Human inventiveness has always been limited by the

11

materials available. In the late Stone Age, Neolithic man invented the bow and arrow. This is generally regarded as the first composite mechanism in that it enabled energy to be stored (by drawing the bow) and rapidly released at will. But with so little knowledge and with only flint available, progress was, quite literally, painfully slow. Neolithic man had to provide himself with new tools before he could really improve his way of life; and, at last, around 4000 BC, he learnt to mine for metals.

Slowly emerging from the age of the stone tool, our ancestors ceased to rely solely on hunting for their food and started to grow it. Farming, the first 'industry', was founded, and communities developed around it. Two great areas of invention were opened up: transport and communication

THE WHEEL

Until now, manpower or muscle power had been the only means of transporting goods. As we can see from the great stone carvings left us by the early Egyptians, almost anything could be moved given a sufficient number of expendable slaves (see figure 4). However, the neighbouring civilisation of Sumer had hit upon a more efficient and less degrading means of transport. With their new-found metal tools they had created the most far-reaching invention of all, the wheel.

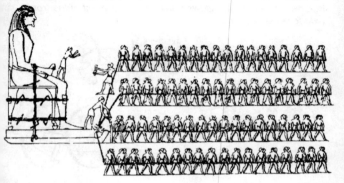

Figure 4: The Egyptian mode of transport before the adoption of the wheel

The first wheels were little more than solid plank discs that rotated with the axle to which they were fixed with wooden pins, but they were good enough. By 3000 BC, in Syria at least, the cart had replaced forever its immediate predecessor, the roller-driven sledge. As the new wheeled vehicle spread to other parts of the world, it gradually became more sophisticated until, by Roman times, with its spoked wheels, stationary axles and steering, its origins were barely recognisable. Yet, in the modern world, when progress in some fields is very rapid, we should remember that this process took no less than two thousand years (*see* figure 5).

In Asia Minor, the potter's wheel was developed and

Figure 5: (a) A sledge with rollers hauled by Neolithic man. (b) Ox-drawn cart, 3000 BC. (c) Roman 4-wheeled carriage drawn by horses. The sway-bar allows horizontal movement of the front axle for easy steering

provided a startling example of *power transmission by rotary motion*. Large-scale extension of this principle, however, had to wait for the invention of the cogged wheel (about 500 BC). Now that one wheel could be 'geared' to drive another, the search began for a 'prime mover', a source of energy independent of human power, to drive it.

THE WATERWHEEL

The cogged wheel, like the lever and the pulley before it, simply translates mechanical energy into a more efficient form. On its own it is quite useless: *it must have power (or energy) to draw upon in the first place*. In the motor car this power is provided by the internal combustion engine, in a wind-up watch by a mainspring.

The Romans sought their prime mover in a combination of the wheel and one of nature's chief sources of energy—running water. The result was the waterwheel, and it was to remain, with the windmill, the only reliable means of feeding power to industry until the introduction of the steam engine in the nineteenth century. In its simplest form it provided an entirely automatic means of milling flour or raising water. In later years it was called upon to drive all manner of machinery, often in large combinations. When engines took over, it was given a new lease of life in the paddle steamer before returning to its original function in the twentieth century, the transmission of energy, as part of the hydro-electric system. So today's waterwheel, instead of turning millstones for flour, drives huge dynamos for the generation of electric current. It has come a long way since 200 BC.

Project

Visit a generating station

As soon as you get the chance, on holiday perhaps, in the Lake District, Scotland or Wales, pay a visit to a modern water-powered generating station. Many of these have a visitor's centre, but if not, do not turn up without first writing for an appointment. That way your trip will not be wasted and you will, no doubt, be guided by an expert.

There are two distinct types of waterwheel. The first is driven by a running stream from *below*, the second by a fall of water from *above* (*see* figure 6). Both transmit their power, as can be seen in the illustration, via a smaller, horizontal, cogged wheel to the grindstones. Which is the more efficient of the two? For many hundreds of years this issue was hotly contested until the English engineer John Smeaton settled all argument with a series of comparative tests in 1759.

Figure 6: (a) Water-powered mill. (b) Overshot watermill. (c) Undershot waterwheel

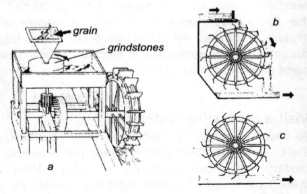

Project

Undershot or overshot?

Why not build a model waterwheel yourself from a construction kit, or hardboard and an epoxy glue, and form your own conclusions? Try and ensure that you use the same volume of water when testing your wheel each time, although you can vary the rate of flow or height of fall as much as you like. Having perfected your 'test tank', compare the number of revolutions your waterwheel makes in one minute according to the overshot and undershot principles. When you are satisfied with your results, check them with those of Smeaton.

PART TWO

THE FORERUNNERS

We shall never know now who invented the lever or the wheel although one thing is certain—they have since been reinvented by many different peoples in many different places. Only as nations developed a higher civilisation for themselves did they begin to *record* their technical achievements and give credit where credit was due. The Greeks led the way.

ARCHIMEDES AND HERO

Archimedes and Hero are the earliest inventors that we know much about. They were scientists and engineers. They had to be. The inventive process is not a cut and dried thing. It needs imagination first, research second and craftsmanship third. With no great fund of scientific knowledge to draw on, all the great inventors, from Archimedes to Galileo, had to do their *own* groundwork.

Today the chief obstacle in the path of an inventor is often a shortage of money. For the pioneers of invention the shortages of data and raw materials were far more serious drawbacks. It is for this reason that their actual achievements are perhaps less striking than those of their successors. But they cannot be underestimated;

their potential was enormous. Figure 7 shows the screw devised by Archimedes to raise water and a working model of a steam turbine attributed to Hero. Both were invented before the birth of Christ but had to wait until the twentieth century and the coming of steel to be widely applied—in the ocean-going liner.

Figure 7: The family tree of an ocean-going liner. (1) The Archimedean screw. (2) Hero's steam engine. (3) The engine pistons and screw of a liner

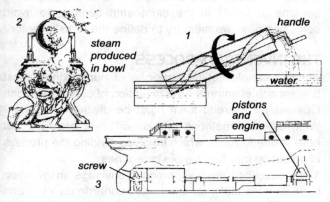

WHO INVENTED WHAT, AND WHEN?

Even with all the facts before us it is not easy to decide the 'true' inventor of *anything*. Indeed, it is the very impossibility of total agreement that makes the question an endless source of fascination, not least to inventors themselves. At the heart of the argument is the simple fact that significant developments are usually *conceived* by one generation, *explored* by another and *developed* by a third. These are three distinct processes, and they may take place centuries apart and in different regions of the world. Hero did not 'invent' the liner, but he certainly made an important contribution. So despite the fact that the split between 'pure' and 'applied' science only really became apparent in the eighteenth century, to avoid confusion now, we must try to define the term 'inventor'.

THE INVENTIVE PROCESS

As an example, let us take one of humankind's most brilliant achievements—the invention of controlled flight. Obviously the credit for it must be divided—but how? Well, different methods provide different answers, but here is one formula, which involves dividing the process of invention into four simple categories:

1 The describer: the first person to envisage an invention in all its essentials, for example, Leonardo da Vinci and the helicopter (1486).

2 The discoverer: the 'pure' scientist; the first person to outline correctly the principles to which a particular invention must conform, for example, Sir George Cayley and the fixed-wing aeroplane (1799).

3 The demonstrator: the first person (usually an engineer and often cited as the inventor proper) to demonstrate the practicality of a particular invention, for example, the Wright brothers and the aeroplane (1903).

4 The developer: the first person to apply an invention to a useful end on a large scale, for example, Sikorsky and the airliner (1913).

Project

Find the inventors

Look at figure 8, where some of the important inventions in history are listed. As you progress through this book, decide who you think should be given credit as the describer, discoverer, demonstrator and developer of each. Then enter their names in the relevant column, as has been done already with the aeroplane.

Two warnings: firstly—use a pencil; you will undoubtedly change your mind on occasion. Secondly— you may be justified in putting *more than one* name in certain spaces and the *same* name in others. There is *no* correct solution, but do compare your answers and the reasoning behind them as widely as possible. There is also great fun to be had in breaking down the categories even further and enlarging your table to take in those developments that are particularly interesting to you— the component parts of the motor car for instance.

Figure 8

locomotive	parachute	steam engine	motor car	aeroplane
				Describer year Sir George Cayley 1799 W. S. Henson 1843 and many others, including Leonardo da Vinci (helicopter only) 1486–90
				Discoverer year Sir George Cayley 1799– John Stringfellow, Alphonse Penaud
				Demonstrator year Orville and Wilbur Wright with powered flight. 17 November 1903
				Developer year Igor Sikorsky with the airliner and the helicopter 1913 1941

THE DARK AGES

By the first century AD the Romans had seized the initiative from the Greeks. They used *their* superior technology to advance an empire. They built the first great roads to improve communications and transport. But, in the end, the ambitions of the Romans outstripped their advances in these fields and led directly to the collapse of their civilisation. As Europe entered the Dark Ages, many of their greatest works—the waterwheel included—disappeared from the face of Britain.

THE PRINTED WORD AND THE RENAISSANCE

The Middle Ages were thus spent in the depressing task of redeveloping a lost technology. Science, like the arts, had to mark time into the fourteenth century and both owe their 'renaissance' (rebirth) largely to the same man: Johann Gutenberg (1397–1468).

As the inventor (demonstrator/developer) of movable type, Gutenberg led a revolution in the art of printing. By the end of the century most of the great books of the world, previously available only in the original and to a privileged few, had been published in their thousands. Scores of *new* books were written, too, not simply for the benefit of the authors' immediate circle, but for the printing presses and the public at large. The impact of this sudden flood of ideas and information throughout

Europe is hard to imagine. One can only record a truly remarkable acceleration in the inventors' rate of progress, which has continued unabated to the present day.

Project

Ingenuity at work

Inventions in the printing industry fall into a rather special category. They owe little to 'pure' science and everything to ingenuity. Take a good look at the inside of a type-

Figure 9: The printing press then and now. (1) Gutenberg-type printing press. (2) Rotary press of the twentieth century

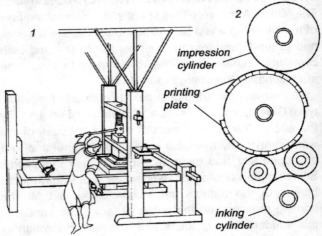

1

2

impression cylinder

printing plate

inking cylinder

writer and it will reveal all its secrets. Then write to your local newspaper and ask for an introduction to its printing works. There you will probably see a modern 'rotary' press. If you watch carefully enough, you should be able to understand its operation with the minimum of explanation from the printer.

LEONARDO DA VINCI AND THE PARACHUTE

At the height of the printing revolution, Leonardo da Vinci (1452–1519)—painter, sculptor, architect, scientist and engineer—was filling notebook after notebook with evidence of his inventive genius.

With remarkable vision, he seriously investigated manned flight and described the helicopter and the tank. He even envisaged the submarine—'an appliance that would enable men to stay some time under water'—but he refused to go into further detail 'because of the evil natures of men who would kill on the sea floor by breaking through the hulls of ships below the water-line . . .'

If Leonardo's dreams were beyond the capacity of fifteenth-century Italy to fulfil, they should at least have proved an inspiration to succeeding generations. But this was not to be. His manuscripts, containing 35,000 words and 500 sketches, were scattered all over Italy and went unpublished for three hundred years.

A miracle of survival

By a miracle, the bulk of Leonardo's manuscripts have survived. Many are in this country and form part of the Royal Collection. Remembering that Leonardo has been called 'the greatest universal genius in history', visit Windsor Castle or the British Museum and examine one of these quite awe-inspiring 'notebooks'.

500 YEARS APART

In figure 10 are three parachutes invented nearly five hundred years apart. The first is that *described* around

Figure 10: Three parachutes: (1) Leonardo's 'rigid tent' parachute (1483). (2) Garnerin's 'parasol' parachute (1797). (3) RAF parachute (1944)

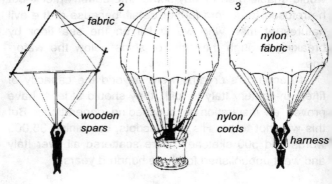

1483 by Leonardo in one of his notebooks: 'If a man have a tent of linen, of which all the apertures have been stopped up, he will be able to throw himself down from any great height without sustaining injury'. The second, based not on the tent but the parasol, was *demonstrated* by a Frenchman, Garnerin, in the first air-to-ground jump (from a balloon at 1000 metres) in 1797. The third is that *developed* by the RAF for use in supersonic aircraft.

Project

Which is the best parachute?

Having made a model of each parachute, it is a simple matter to conduct comparative tests—from a kite (*see* figure 31). Figure 11 shows how this is done. The

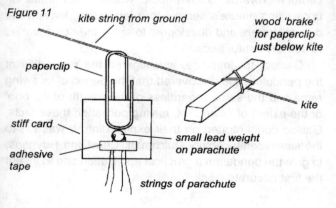

Figure 11

kite string from ground

wood 'brake' for paperclip just below kite

paperclip

kite

stiff card

small lead weight on parachute

adhesive tape

strings of parachute

parachute, attached to a paperclip, is borne up the kite's string from ground level under air pressure. When it reaches the 'stop' (attached to the kite's string before sending it aloft), the 'chute' is torn free of the paperclip by the wind and begins its descent. Meanwhile, the paperclip itself returns to the bottom of the string ready for the next parachute.

GALILEO AND THE MECHANICAL CLOCK

If Leonardo was primarily a describer, his fellow Italian, Galilei Galileo (1564–1642), was a *discoverer*, a 'pure' scientist, a mathematician and astronomer, just like Archimedes had been before him. From the sixteenth century onwards, such people would concentrate on unravelling nature's secrets in a laboratory, leaving the demonstrators and developers to apply their discoveries to socially useful ends.

Galileo, for instance, investigated the properties of the pendulum. He discovered that the period of its swing remained the same regardless of the weight of its 'bob' or the extent of its arc. Yet, having published these facts, Galileo concentrated on their explanation. It was left to the seventeenth-century Dutchman, Christiaan Huygens, to give the pendulum a practical application and to invent the first accurate clock.

Project

The swing of the pendulum

Make a pendulum 100 centimetres (39 inches) in length with a fairly heavy 'bob'. How long does it take to complete one full swing? To obtain a swing of a different duration should you:

1 alter the weight of the bob?
2 alter the 'amplitude' (or arc) of the swing?
3 alter the length of the pendulum itself?

Project

Which is the best time-keeper?

Before the introduction of mechanical clocks people kept

Figure 12: Three primitive clocks: (1) Sundial. (2) Water clock. (3) Candle clock

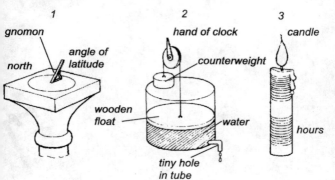

track of time with such primitive clocks as those shown in figure 12. Devise your own version of:

1 a sundial

2 a candle clock

3 a water clock.

Which is the most accurate over a period of:

1 15 minutes?

2 60 seconds?

Can you counter the disadvantages inherent in each of these clocks or improve their accuracy?

PART THREE

A REVOLUTION IN INDUSTRY

Throughout the Renaissance the whole of western Europe had been stockpiling ideas and information beyond its technology to apply to useful ends. It earned for the seventeenth century the title of 'The Age of Projects'. Yet one country was ready to step up the action. Britain was ripe for what we now call the Industrial Revolution. For a time Britain alone had the money (thanks to peace at home and a policy of free trade abroad) and a large, skilled labour force. Above all, she had a new breed of inventor—dour, persistent men combining the practicality of the craftsman with the imagination and ambition of the merchant venturers who were by now engaged in building an empire overseas.

A NEW 'PRIME MOVER'

The Industrial Revolution of the eighteenth century was triggered by the development of the first significant prime mover since the waterwheel and the windmill. The *steam engine* had many advantages over its predecessors, but the most obvious was its portability. It could do its work anywhere. It did not need a river and it did not need a wind. If its energy could be harnessed, scores of people could be released from drudgery for more rewarding work, as others had been freed before them by the wheel. The power of steam to accomplish such a miracle had been recognised since Archimedes's day. In figure 13 is a model of a device described by Hero 'for the opening and shutting of the temple doors'. It was a perfectly practical proposition. The fire on the altar causes the air contained beneath it to *expand* and expel the water from a closed tank into a bucket—which thereupon descended under its own weight and opened the doors. When the fire was doused, the air cooled and, having contracted, sucked the water back into the tank to close the doors again. Hey presto!

Project

Build a model

Examine the model of Hero's device in figure 13 carefully. Then, when you are sure you understand the principle involved, ask your science teacher if you could build it in the lab to demonstrate its practicality. The method of construction and the choice of materials is left to you, the inventor.

THE STEAM ENGINE COMES OF AGE

Throughout the sixteenth and seventeenth centuries many of the greatest inventors, Leonardo included,

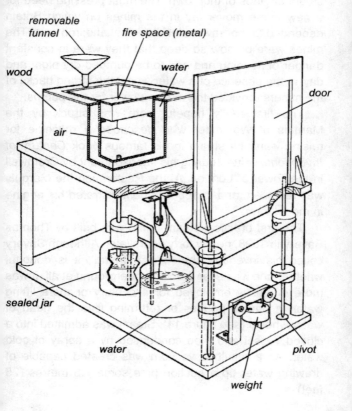

Figure 13: How steam opened and closed the doors of a Greek temple (100 AD)

removable funnel

fire space (metal)

wood

water

door

air

sealed jar

water

pivot

weight

followed in Hero's footsteps and experimented with steam engines of their own. The most pressing need for a new prime mover lay in the mines on which Britain depended for her raw materials—coal and iron ores. The mines were by now so deep that they were in constant danger of flooding and had to be pumped dry night and day. In the absence of a water wheel the strong backs of the miners provided the motive power for the pumps.

The first really hopeful note was struck by the Marquis of Worcester who *described* a machine for raising water by steam in his famous book *Century of Inventions*, written during his imprisonment by Cromwell in the Tower of London. At the Restoration the Marquis was released, and in 1660 he *demonstrated* his engine in model form.

The first practical steam pump was built by Thomas Savery in 1698, nearly forty years later. Although Savery called his invention 'the miner's friend', it is doubtful whether one was ever erected underground at all. It was more modestly employed for a century or more lifting water in private houses or returning it to the head of water wheels (*see* figure 14). Steam was admitted into a closed vessel and then condensed by a spray of cold water. As a result, a vacuum was created capable of drawing water up a suction pipe some 7.5 metres (25 feet).

Figure 14: Savery's steam pump (1702)

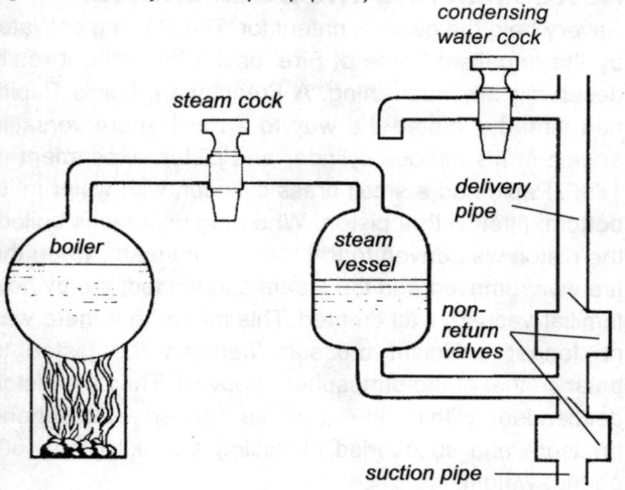

Project

Make a comparison

Compare Savery's 'engine' (figure 14) with Hero's (figure 13) on page 33. They are separated by at least sixteen hundred years, but the principle employed is much the same. Where, then, do the differences lie and what might account for the painfully slow progress of the steam engine thus far?

NEWCOMEN AND THE BEAM ENGINE

Savery held the general patent for 'The Raising of Water by the Impellent Force of Fire' until 1733 without really deserving any such thing. A Frenchman, Denis Papin, had already pointed the way to a much more versatile engine in his famous cylinder and piston experiment of 1690. Papin had a small brass cylinder, with water in its bottom, fitted with a piston. When the water was boiled, the piston was driven to the top by the steam; when the fire was removed and the steam condensed, the by now familiar vacuum was created. This meant that there was no longer sufficient pressure *beneath* the piston to balance that of the atmosphere *above* it. Thus the piston descended within the cylinder under atmospheric pressure and succeeded in raising a 27-kilogram (60-pound) weight.

Papin died unnoticed and in abject poverty sometime around 1712. Meanwhile, an ironmonger from Dartmouth, Thomas Newcomen (1663–1729), had transformed his model of the 'atmospheric' engine into a really practical prime mover. In 1712 the first of thousands of Newcomen Beam Engines was erected at a colliery near Dudley Castle, Staffordshire. Figure 15, based on a contemporary engraving, shows the engine in fascinating detail. An open-ended cylinder is supplied with steam from a brick boiler. The piston, packed with

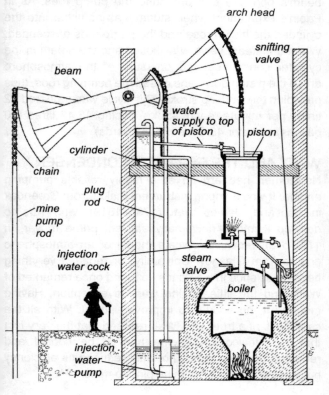

Figure 15: Newcomen's atmospheric beam engine of 1712. The figure on the left gives a splendid indication of the sheer size of Newcomen's masterpiece.

leather and sealed with a layer of water on top, is hung by a chain from the arch head of a rocking beam. At the beam's opposite end are hung the pump rods. As in Papin's experiment when steam was admitted into the cylinder, the piston rose and the pump rods descended. When the steam valve was closed and the steam in the cylinder condensed, the pressure of the atmosphere drove the piston down and raised the pumping rods, thus providing the working stroke. This cycle was repeated 12 times per minute, each 'stroke' raising 45.46 litres (10 gallons) of water 46.6 metres (51 yards).

WATT AND THE SEPARATE CONDENSER

Newcomen had arrived at a highly reliable pumping engine. It was a young instrument maker from Greenock in Scotland, James Watt (1736–1819), who was to *develop* it into a universally efficient prime mover. In 1763 Watt received a scale model of an atmospheric engine from Glasgow University for repair. 'Everything became science in his hands,' a friend once remarked of Watt, and the little engine was no exception. Having mended it, he sought to improve upon it. With all the canniness of a true Scot, Watt realised that the very fact that the Newcomen engine had to be cooled and reheated *at every stroke* not only reduced its efficiency but wasted the coal it was helping to mine.

Watt has himself recorded how he came to invent the greatest single improvement to the steam engine, the separate condenser. 'I perceived,' he wrote, 'that in order to make the best use of steam it was necessary— first, that the cylinder should be maintained *always as hot as the steam which entered it*; and, secondly, that when the steam was condensed, the water of which it was composed . . . should be cooled down. The means of accomplishing these points did not immediately present themselves; but early in 1765 it occurred to me that if a communication were opened between a cylinder containing steam and another vessel exhausted of air and other fluids the steam, as an elastic fluid, would immediately rush into the empty vessel . . . and if that vessel were kept very cool by an injection, more steam would continue to enter until the whole was condensed.' Figure 16 on page 40 shows the theory and practice of Watt's separate condenser.

Watt joined forces with the great Birmingham manufacturer, Matthew Boulton, and together they built a series of engines that revolutionised not only Britain's industry but much of the world's. They charged the colliery owners a royalty on every ton of coal saved over the old Newcomen engines and used the money to finance further improvements. In his patent of 1781 Watt took the most important step of all. By the 'sun and

Figure 16: The theory and practice of Watt's separate condenser

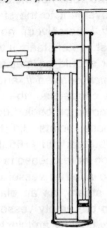

planet' movement of a set of gear wheels (*see* figure 17) he turned the reciprocating action of his engine into a rotary one.

The following year he went one step further and made his new engine 'double acting' by admitting steam above as well as below the piston so that it no longer relied upon atmospheric pressure for its downward, or 'working'. stroke. Now the steam engine could not only go anywhere but do anything, or so it must have seemed in the nineteenth century. As her countrymen left the

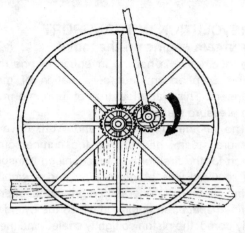

Figure 17: Rotary action—the 'sun and planet' system. By what other means might James Watt have obtained rotary action?

fields for the factories, Britain switched her dependence from agriculture to the new manufacturing industries. Great new cities grew like mushrooms in the night, and a second revolution was born in the field of transport. The days of the horse and carriage were numbered. The railways were coming!

PART FOUR

A REVOLUTION IN TRANSPORT
The steam engine on the move

'The locomotive is not the invention of one man,' said Robert Stephenson, 'but of a nation of mechanical engineers.' This was most true of its prime mover—the high pressure steam engine.

The engines of Boulton and Watt, driven by low pressure steam, had proved too cumbersome in the search for the first form of mechanised transport. What was required was a *light* engine and a *small* one, an engine capable of generating a great deal of energy *in a confined space*; an engine in which the cylinder was so finely bored, the piston so tightly sealed and the boiler so soundly constructed as to withstand high pressure steam.

While such an engine was still being developed, Joseph Cugnot, a French artillery officer, built the first ever mechanically driven vehicle using a gun carriage for his chassis (figure 18). After painfully slow trials it ran wild and was locked up in the national arsenal out of harm's way. In 1801 Richard Trevithick, a Cornish mining engineer, became the first man to *demonstrate* a high pressure steam carriage capable of operating at an average speed above that of conventional horse-drawn

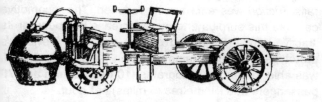

Figure 18: Cugnot's steam-driven gun carriage (1769)

vehicles. 'Puffing Devil', as she was christened, went up in flames after her first public outing, but two years later Trevithick drove her successor all the way from Cornwall to London.

However, a campaign had been mounted in the meantime opposing the development of 'travelling engines' as dangerous to pedestrians and damaging to the highway. When no less a figure than James Watt (who it should be said had his *own* plans for a steam carriage) joined the ranks of his opponents, Trevithick compromised. Having put the high pressure steam engine on wheels, he set the whole on cast-iron rails, which had been in use at pit-heads since 1767. It is this simple step above all others that entitles Trevithick to be regarded as 'The Father of The Railway'.

Project

Make a 'dynamometer'

Social considerations aside, there was a practical

advantage to be gained by putting the steam engine on rails: *friction* was enormously reduced. The locomotive can use this surplus energy to increase its speed or its 'tractive effort'—i.e. pulling power—and even Trevithick's prototype of 1803, running from Pen-y-Darran to Cardiff, was able to haul 900 kilograms (10 tons) of iron and 70 passengers at 8 kilometres (5 miles) per hour.

Tractive effort is measured by a *dynamometer*. The one shown in figure 19 can be made in a matter of minutes and hitched between any model train (electric or clockwork) and its rolling stock.

1 If the engine's load is doubled, is its *tractive effort* halved? If not, why not?

2 Is your engine more efficient with a heavy load:

(a) all in *one* goods wagon?

(b) divided between several wagons?

Figure 19: How to make a dynamometer

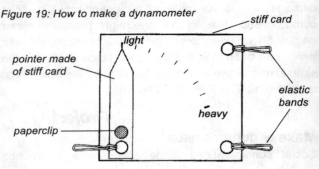

44

3 If you can run your engine independently of its rails, to what degree is its tractive effort impaired:

(a) on the carpet?

(b) on a smooth surface?

In 1808 Richard Trevithick *demonstrated* his second locomotive, 'Catch me who can', on an specially built track in the heart of London (*see* figure 20). This attempt at popularising steam traction—at a shilling (5p) a ride—

Figure 20: Trevithick's 'Catch me who can' in Euston Square, London (1808)

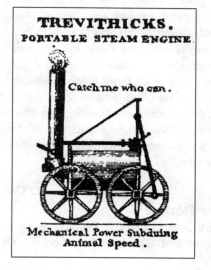

TREVITHICKS.
PORTABLE STEAM ENGINE.

Catch me who can.

Mechanical Power Subduing
Animal Speed.

was a great success with the public but left hard-headed industrialists and politicians unmoved. One day a rail broke and the engine overturned. Trevithick was forced to sell his patent to feed his family, and in 1816 he sailed for South America to work in the gold and silver mines of Peru, leaving the field clear for another man to reap the fame and fortune of his invention—George Stephenson. Today the two men, *demonstrator* and *developer* of the locomotive railway, share a memorial window with Isambard Kingdom Brunel in Westminster Abbey.

The Rainhill Trials were held to select a locomotive for the first major railway in the world, the Liverpool and Manchester. George Stephenson, who had built the line, won a convincing victory with his son Robert's 'Rocket' over his competitors, 'Novelty' and 'Sanspareil'.

In the case of all three locomotives, the piston now powered the leading wheel, not the axle, and its reciprocating action was transformed into rotary motion by a *crank*. Stephenson's method of connecting the piston rod to the crank was, however, unique and contributed to his victory.

Project

See the 'Rocket'

If you are able to visit the Science Museum in London, the 'Rocket' and 'Sanspareil' will speak for themselves.

THE PNEUMATIC RAILWAY

In sorry contrast to the 'Rocket', the last steam locomotive to be built for British Rail—'Evening Star', No. 92220—was scrapped in 1965. She had been in service for just five years. Diesel and electric trains became the order of the day, and speeds in excess of 160 kph (100 mph) became commonplace. Yet none of these developments can compare with the prospect held out by some of an updated version of the 'pneumatic railway' invented in the reign of Queen Victoria.

In 1864, T. W. Rammell, a tireless advocate of 'pneumatic traction', successfully *demonstrated* his passenger-carrying 'tube train' in the grounds of the Crystal Palace. A saloon coach, encircled by a ring of bristles in order to ensure an airtight joint, was blown and sucked to and fro in a 548-metre (600-yard) tunnel. Progress in other fields, such as the internal combustion engine, and lack of finance were all that prevented the large-scale application of Rammell's invention.

Project

Build your own pneumatic railway

You can build your own pneumatic railway (*see* figure 21) with a short length of hose, preferably transparent, and a garden pump of the kind used for spraying roses. Use your pneumatic tube as a test-bed for trains of

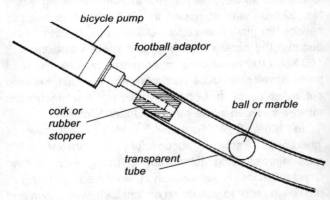

Figure 21: Build your own pneumatic 'test-bed'. (Note that a bicycle pump will do, but unless it can be adapted to suck as well as blow, it will only provide a one-way service.)

bicycle pump

football adaptor

cork or rubber stopper

ball or marble

transparent tube

varying size, shape, weight and construction. Can you combine high speed and reliability with a really practical design?

THE HORSELESS CARRIAGE AND THE INTERNAL-COMBUSTION ENGINE

The canal owners of Britain fought long and hard to prevent the spread of the railway. Where they failed, those with a vested interest in the horse and carriage met with some success. Before the 'horseless carriage' could catch the imagination of the public, its opponents prompted Parliament into subjecting it to crippling tolls and a speed limit of 6.5 kph (4 mph)!

As often happens in such cases, Britain surrendered her initiative in the development of mechanised road transport to others. The steam engine was abandoned in favour of a lighter prime mover. In 1876 in Germany Nikolaus Otto patented an engine based on a principle originally *described* by Denis Papin and *demonstrated* by Etienne Lenoir. Whereas the steam engine burnt coal in a boiler, its successor mixed gas or petrol with air and burnt it inside the cylinder itself. The internal-combustion engine is still with us over one hundred years later in much the same form as that devised by Otto. Its four-stroke cycle is illustrated in figure 22:

1 *Suction* of the fuel/air mixture into the cylinder where a partial vacuum has been created by the downward thrust of the piston.

2 *Compression* of the mixture as soon as the inlet valve is closed by the re-bounding piston..

3 *Ignition* of the mixture by an electric spark; the mixture 'explodes' and the piston is driven down by the expanding gases. This is the power stroke.

4 *Expulsion* of the burnt gas by the rebounding piston via the outlet valve.

Otto designed his engine for the factory floor. It was to run on gas drawn from the mains supply. It was meant

Figure 22: Suck, squeeze, bang and blow—the four strokes of the internal combustion engine

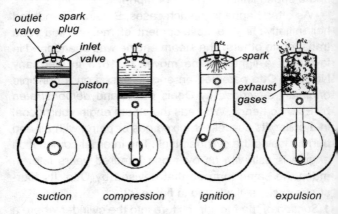

suction   *compression*   *ignition*   *expulsion*

to stay where it was. Yet two other German engineers saw in the internal combustion engine the ideal prime mover for a new form of road transport. Only 95 kilometres (60 miles) apart and quite independently of each other, they set about putting the internal-combustion engine on wheels. Both came to the conclusion that it should run on petrol. Both introduced ignition by electric spark, and both *demonstrated* their finished product in 1885. Neither machine was a car as we know it. Benz's tricycle and Daimler's motorcycle were prototypes and soon improved upon. The design of the motor car initially aped the horsedrawn cab. As such, it was less than stable. Look at figure 23. The centre of gravity of the Benz is much too high, and it is clearly in danger of tipping over if it corners at any great speed. The Model 'T' Ford, mass-produced twenty years later in America, is a great improvement. With her low centre of gravity she offered much less wind resistance than the Benz and as a consequence combined greater speed with greater safety. 'Tin Lizzie', as she became known, remained on the market until 1927. Fifteen million were sold and by 1914 the price was down to £100. The motor car was no longer to be thought of as a carriage without the horses but as a vehicle designed in her own right and

Figure 23: Design comparison of: (1) The Benz tricycle (1888). (2) The Model 'T' Ford—Tin Lizzie (1908)

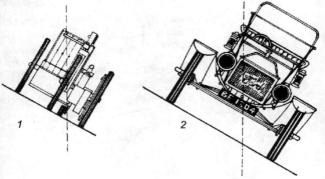

one of the most important machines of the twentieth century.

Project

Build a go-kart

Figure 24 should enable you to build a simple go-kart with an adjustable steering board. The latter will allow you to vary the distance between the front and rear wheels for maximum stability. Can you incorporate into this basic design:

1 A brake for the rear wheels?
2 Wheel steering?
3 Springing?

Figure 24: A simple go-kart

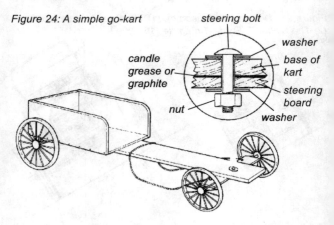

Make an accelerometer

The simple instrument in figure 25, made from a piece of curtain rod and a marble, will measure the rate of acceleration and deceleration of any car, train, plane or even your newly constructed go-kart. The faster the vehicle in which it is placed accelerates, the farther the marble will roll *in the opposite direction*. On the other hand, deceleration (braking) will cause the marble to roll *forward*. The accelerometer's twin scales will provide you with readings. Make an accelerometer for yourself and for a start try comparing the performance of different cars in different gears.

Figure 25: A simple accelerometer

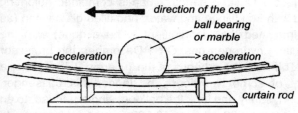

MANNED FLIGHT

Manned flight has been a fiercely competitive sphere of invention from the outset. The balloon and the spaceship have that much in common.

Had the inventor of the hot-air balloon, Laurenco de Gusmao, a Jesuit priest, not lived in fear of the Inquisition, he might well have flown before his death in 1724. As it was, *lighter-than-air* flight came to its climax in 1783, one hundred years before the invention of the automobile. On 21 November a vast crowd gathered in Paris to witness two noblemen, Pilâtre de Rozier and the Marquis d'Arlandes, earn their place in history as the *first men to fly*. Their hot-air balloon, built by the Montgolfièr brothers, attained a height of 1000 metres (3000 feet) and flew for eight kilometres (five miles) over Paris.

It had taken human beings thousands of years to attain free flight. Yet within two weeks, the Montgolfièrs' achievement was eclipsed by a popular scientist, Professor César Charles. Charles combined sulphuric acid with iron filings and water, and filled his balloon (as he imagined the Montgolfièrs to have done) with the resulting hydrogen gas. On 1 December, the professor took off from the grounds of the Tuileries Palace. After a flight of some two hours, he landed his passenger, Robert, safely and took the balloon, single-handed, to an altitude of 3,220 metres (10,560 feet). On his return to Paris, the hydrogen balloon had won the day, and he himself was acclaimed in the manner we now reserve for those who go to the moon.

A comparison of the two first people-carrying

Figure 26: A comparison of: (1) The Montgolfière hot-air balloon (2) The Charlière hydrogen balloon

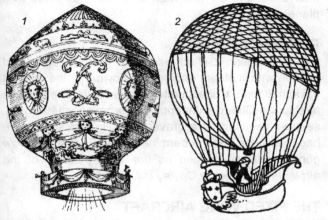

balloons shows the Charlière to be altogether superior to its rival (figure 26). The gondola's weight is evenly distributed by the net; sandbags provide ballast, giving the pilot some control over ascent; the gas-escape valve regulates the balloon's landing. The Montgolfière relies entirely on its dangerous gondola-borne furnace.

Balloon flight has a sad as well as a glorious parallel with space flight. In 1785, only two years after becoming the first aeronaut, Pilâtre de Rozier was killed when a balloon of his own design, a combination of the Charlière and the Montgolfière, crashed in an attempt to cross the

English Channel. In 1968, Yuri Gagarin, only seven years after becoming the first man in space, was killed in a plane crash.

POWERED FLIGHT
By 1852, Henri Giffard had fitted out an elongated balloon with a steam engine and flown into the wind at 9.5 kph (6 mph) to inaugurate powered flight. The dirigible airship, as Giffard's unhappy compromise was termed, seemed destined for a brave future. In fact, that future had long since been undermined by an Englishman now generally acknowledged as the 'true' inventor of the airplane—Sir George Cayley (1773-1857).

THE FIXED WING AIRCRAFT
Throughout history *heavier-than-air* flight had been

Figure 27: Ornithopter designed by Leonardo da Vinci (c.1500)

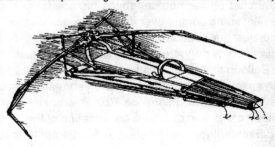

discussed solely in terms of 'ornithopters' (figure 27). The designers of such machines, in the hope of imitating bird flight, relied on various flap-wing devices to provide *both* lift *and* forward motion. Cayley's genius lay in his ability to divorce these two functions. In his earliest design of 1799 he advocated a *fixed wing* to supply lift and *propellers*, driven by a light engine, to provide thrust. In the most stupendous statement in the history of aeronautics, he wrote: 'The whole problem is confined within these limits, to make a surface support a given weight by the application of power to the resistance of air.' (*See* figure 28.)

Figure 28: The forces acting on an aeroplane–thrust must overcome drag; lift must overcome weight

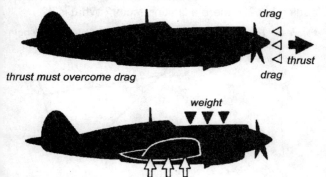

The aerodynamics of the kite

The kite provides the best means of identifying the forces involved in mechanised flight. The one shown in figure 29 is made from a man's pocket handkerchief and can be launched in a moderate wind. Look again at figure 28. From what source does a kite get: (a) its thrust, (b) its lift?

What function does the kite's tail perform? What is the aeroplane's equivalent? Can you succeed in flying the kite *without* a tail? Can you fly it with the 'warped' surface facing the ground? How many more such kites can you send up in tandem, i.e. flying from the *same* line several hundred metres apart? How high can you fly the leading kite? Is there a limiting factor? What is it?

Figure 29: How to make a pocket handkerchief kite. Each length of dowel should be cut slightly longer than the diagonal of the handkerchief in order to provide 'warp'.

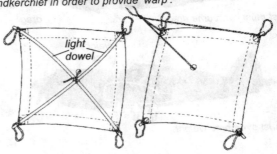

light
dowel

THE AEROPLANE TAKES SHAPE

In 1809 Cayley founded the science of aerodynamics by publishing his concept of fixed wing flight. No one took it at all seriously, and it was left to Cayley himself to subject it to a really vigorous examination. Using a whirling arm of his own invention, he tested the lifting capacities of various wing shapes and incorporated his findings into full-sized gliders. The last and most sophisticated of these contained the following features:

1 fixed cambered wings, dihedrally opposed for lateral stability,

2 an adjustable tailplane for longitudinal stability,

3 a pilot-operated rudder for directional stability,

4 a lightweight cycle-type undercarriage.

Cayley's granddaughter has left us an eye-witness account of this machine's maiden flight. The year is 1853 and Cayley is 80 years old:

'The coachman went in the machine and landed on the west side at about the same level. I think it came down rather a shorter distance than expected. The coachman got himself clear, and when the watchers had got across, he shouted, "Please, Sir George, I wish to give notice. I was hired to drive, and not to fly . . ." That's all I recollect. The machine was put high away in the barn, and I used to sit and hide in it when so inspired.'

Sir George himself never doubted the ultimate

triumph of the fixed wing aeroplane once it could command sufficient thrust. Ninety-four years before the Wright brothers proved him right, Cayley put his vision on record and predicted the means by which sustained and controlled flight would eventually be made possible —the petrol engine:

'I feel perfectly confident that it will be possible to transport persons and goods more securely by air than by water, with a velocity from 20 to 100 miles [32 to 160 kilometres] an hour. It is only necessary to develop a suitable engine. Boulton-Watt's steam engine might be a possible source of power, but as lightness is of so much value, there is the probability of using the expansion of the air by sudden combustion of inflammable powders or fluids.'

Project

The Wright brothers

The Wright brothers, having mastered lateral control, beat the rest of the world into the air by some five years. On 17 December 1903, they took it in turns to pilot the first machine in history to take off under its own power in sustained and controlled flight.

The Wrights' plane was all the more remarkable for being entirely of their own design and construction. They built their own petrol engine and shaped their own

*Figure 30: A design comparison of: (1) The Wright Flyer (1907).
(2) The Spirit of St Louis (1927)*

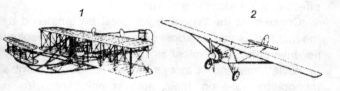

propellers. The first airplane was christened 'The Flyer'
—a simple statement of fact. In figure 30 its design is
compared with that of another famous American plane,
'The Spirit of St Louis', with which Lindbergh flew the
Atlantic single-handed in 1927.

THE WRIGHT 'FLYER' AND 'THE SPIRIT OF ST LOUIS'

Despite the totally different arrangement of the two
machines, the most startling contrast lies in their relative
systems of lateral ('banking') control. This is effected in
'The Flyer' by the differential twisting—or *'warping'*—of
the wing tips by a complex series of cables. In 'The Spirit
of St Louis' the same effect is achieved much more
simply by *ailerons*. Longitudinal control (climbing and
diving) is the job of the *elevator*. 'The Flyer' has a huge
elevator perched ahead of the wings and twin propellers
immediately behind them. The elevators on Lindbergh's

plane are where we would expect to find them today—in the tailplane. Directional control on both machines is effected by a *rudder* at the rear.

Criticism of the Wright 'Flyer' must be tempered by the fact that its cumbersome design is the direct result of its inventors' determination to build an 'inherently unstable' machine. Cayley's gliders and Lindbergh's monoplane rely on their aerodynamic lines for a measure of built-in (inherent) stability. The Wrights' biplane does not. Its lateral and longitudinal stability is governed at all times by its controls and the pilot operating them. Can you suggest why the Wright brothers rejected an inherently stable design?

PART FIVE

A REVOLUTION IN COMMUNICATIONS

Living as we do in an age when pictures as well as voices can be relayed from the moon right into our living rooms, we tend to take good communications for granted. Similarly, now that facts and figures, sounds and images can be stored forever in a computer or on tape, it is not easy for us to appreciate what an impact the sound of his or her own voice reproduced on a 'talking machine' must have made on a Victorian. Perhaps the only way to put the communications revolution in its proper perspective is to imagine ourselves back in the nineteenth century and to reinvent the electronic means by which information was first relayed and the human voice preserved.

THE MORSE TELEGRAPH AND 'INSTANT COMMUNICATION'

In 1800, when the courier was still the standard means of long-distance communication, the Italian physicist Count Volta published his *discovery* that continuous flow of 'electric fluid' could be maintained by chemical means. Such a circuit, maintained by a relay of primitive batteries, was established when Samuel Morse linked

Washington and Baltimore by overhead wire in 1844. Although not the first means of 'instant communication', it was by far the simplest. Its messages were borne by the 'electric fluid' along the wires by the practice of opening and closing the circuit according to a carefully formulated pattern of long and short signals—the dashes and dots of the Morse code.

Project

Be a telegraphist

The Morse telegraph in figure 31 will transmit your coded messages from one room to another. Apart from the 6-

Figure 31: How to make a Morse telegraph of 1837

dots								dashes							
Ė								T̄							
•• Ï			•— Ā				—• N̄				—— M̄				
••• S	••— U	•—• R	•—— W	—•• D	—•— K	——• G	——— O								
H	V	F		L		P	J	B	X	C	Y	Z	Q		

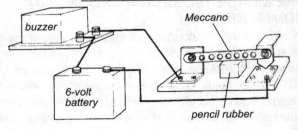

buzzer

Meccano

6-volt battery

pencil rubber

volt battery and buzzer, it requires only a few pieces of Meccano, plenty of wire and a soft pencil rubber.

The Morse code itself is included in its most easily deciphered form. If on first examination it appears confusing, look again. It is, in fact, logical enough.

The first telegram carried by the 'Washington/Baltimore telegraph' was transmitted by Morse himself from the Supreme Court. It read:

•––/•••• /•–/–   ••••/•–/–/••••

––•/–––/– ••   •––/•–•/–––/••–/––•/••••/–

(What hath God wrought)

THE TINFOIL PHONOGRAPH AND 'THE INDUSTRY OF HUMAN HAPPINESS'

The first to *capture and preserve* sound was a young American telegraph tycoon, Thomas Edison. His talking machine of 1877 had its beginnings in the permanent record the Morse telegraph made of its messages.

Instead of cutting dots and dashes in a strip of paraffin paper (as the telegraph did), Edison's phonograph recorded the vibrations of the human voice in *one continuous scratch* of varying depth on a cylinder wrapped in tinfoil. The prototype is said to have been built in one day and to have launched what its inventor termed 'the industry of human happiness' with the words: 'Mary had a little lamb . . .'

The record-player as we know it today is descended from the disc gramophone invented by Emil Berliner in 1887. Edison continued to release everything from pop to opera on cylinders until 1929 when his machine reverted to its original role, that of a dictation machine. The cylinder still lives on in such machines today—most notably in 'The Dictaphone'.

Project

Following in Edison's footsteps

The Edison recorder in figure 32 is based on its

Figure 32: How to make Edison's tinfoil recorder of 1877

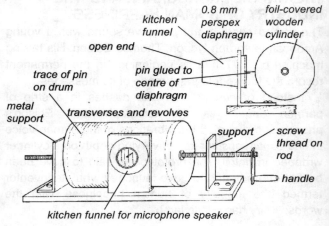

inventor's tinfoil prototype of 1877. As such, it may take a little trial and error before you are able to preserve the sound of your own voice in the following manner:

1 Wind the cylinder as far to the right as it will go.

2 Speaking directly into the funnel, wind the cylinder to the left. Maintain a steady rate.

3 Rewind the cylinder to the right very gently so that the needle does not spoil your recording.

4 Play back your recording by winding the cylinder to the left.

PART SIX

TOMORROW'S INVENTORS

Progress in the twentieth century has been so rapid that the output of its inventors exceeds that of its predecessors throughout the whole of history. Whether we like it or not, the tide seems irreversible. Given the right 'materials' and 'data' by the scientists and their computers, the inventors of tomorrow will continue to change the face of the world. Their responsibility, and ours, will be to see that those changes do not create more problems than they overcome.

If, having explored through these pages the inventions of others, you have any bright ideas of your own, you should write to the Institute of Patentees and Inventors at Suite 505a, Triumph House, 189 Regent Street, London W1R 7WF.

To qualify for a patent an invention must have: (a) a function, (b) an end product, and (c) at least one *original aspect* (whether or not it combines existing components). It must not be frivolous or illegal.

LET'S INVESTIGATE!

Titles in this series: